MAXIMIZE YOUR MARRIAGE

T0321577

MAXIMIZE YOUR MARRIAGE

The Biblical Foundations for Marriage

Donald Wikoff, M.D.

ELM HILL

A Division of
HarperCollins Christian Publishing

www.elmhillbooks.com

Maximize your Marriage

The Biblical Foundations for Marriage

Published in Nashville, Tennessee, by Elm Hill, an imprint of Thomas Nelson. Elm Hill and Thomas Nelson are registered trademarks of HarperCollins Christian Publishing, Inc.

Elm Hill titles may be purchased in bulk for educational, business, fund-raising, or sales promotional use. For information, please e-mail SpecialMarkets@ ThomasNelson.com.

Library of Congress Cataloging-in-Publication Data

Library of Congress Control Number: 2018961838

ISBN 978-0-310101987 (Paperback)
ISBN 978-0-310101994 (Hardbound)
ISBN 978-0-310102007 (eBook)

CONTENT

Content

Introductory Remarks

Before we wade into a study of the Bible and what it has to say about marriage, let me give you some introductory observations from scripture that we will develop in our study. This is somewhat like a *Cliff Notes* version which gives us a very short but reflective view of the whole study. Nine observations follow; they are:

1. **GOD** instituted and designed marriage!
2. He did **not** design it to be easy!
3. Opposites attract (there's a reason)
4. **God rigged the system!**
5. Men and women are **very** different!
6. God loves sandpaper! (Hint: You have a hand in picking the grit grade of paper)
7. Glorious success is possible!
8. Marriage (and family) is just a physically tangible manifestation of a heavenly relationship, created to provide insight into every aspect of the heavenly, divine, spiritual marriage of Christ and the church.
9. **Love is a choice, not a feeling!**

This will give you the general direction we are headed. To facilitate review of the scriptures we will study, as we work through maximizing our marriages, the Bible references that form the skeleton upon which all observations are made are listed at the end of the book. Read, ponder, assimilate, and instigate these scriptures to maximize your marriage. God bless you in your endeavor! The fact that you have even read this far means you have an interest in seeing your marriage improve. It will be my prayer that the Biblical perspectives which follow will revolutionize you, your spouse, your marriage, your family, and your impact on those in your sphere of influence! Now to get started!

CHAPTER ONE

To understand the foundations of Biblical marriage, one has to start with the institution of marriage, understand by whom it was instituted, and for what purpose. The characteristics of marriage as intended by God are described for us in the book of beginnings, the book of Genesis. So let us begin to cultivate our understanding of marriage by seeing what God had to say about marriage when He first instituted it in the Garden of Eden. As you probably know, Genesis is the first book of the Bible, and the first book of the Pentateuch. The Pentateuch is the first five books of the Bible as written by Moses. The foundations for all of our Christian beliefs are formed in the Pentateuch, particularly Genesis. Let us begin our search for understanding in **Genesis 1:26–28, NIV.**

> **26 Then God said, "Let us make man in our image, in our likeness, and let them rule over the fish of the sea and the birds of the air, over the livestock, over all the earth, and over all the creatures that move along the ground."**
>
> **27 So God created man in his own image,**
> **in the image of God he created him;**
> **male and female he created them.**
> **28 God blessed them and said to them, "Be fruitful and increase in number; fill the earth and subdue it. Rule over the**

fish of the sea and the birds of the air and over every living creature that moves on the ground."

First, notice that it reads, "Let us...," so who is us? This is a plural pronoun, and is the first indication in the Bible of the trinity. We are given to understand in the rest of the Bible that the trinity is composed of the Father, the Son, and the Holy Spirit. Thus, the collaborative decision was made in heaven to make man. And how was he to be made? In the image and likeness of the members of the trinity. To be made in their image and likeness means that we share the characteristics of all three. It means that we can be identified as coming from them because we bear their characteristics. Next, God, through Moses, shares the assignment for man. It is to rule. Rule over the whole of all living birds, fish, and animals. God then gave a directive that in addition to ruling, males and females were to utilize their sexuality to have children and to fill the earth with mankind. Man has seemed to do a pretty good job of this command, as there are now 7.5 billion people on the earth. So, in the Garden of Eden, in a place of utopia, God had a purpose for males and females, to be fruitful, to multiply, to fill, to subdue, and to rule. He gave more direction in Genesis 2:15.

Gen 2:15-16

15 The Lord God took the man and put him in the Garden of Eden to work it and take care of it.

So man was given work to do! Yes, in the perfect environment, in fellowship with God, and living in a place of unspoiled beauty, God intended for man to work! This is before the fall, and it is evident that work was a privilege and a blessing as directed by God.

What does this have to do with marriage, you ask? The answer is that God gave Adam a task too big for him to manage by himself. God declares in Genesis 2:18:

Gen 2:18

18 The Lord God said, "It is not good for the man to be alone. I will make a helper suitable for him."

Was it not good for man to be alone because man was not created adequately? Was Adam somehow a flawed creation? Actually, God tells us in Genesis 1:31, the day he made man and woman, that not only was his creative effort that day good, it was the only day of the six days of creation which God ended by saying it was very good. So, no, Adam was not flawed as though his creation was lacking in some respect; rather, God was more proud of his creation of man and woman than he was of the rest of creation.

God has acknowledged that despite a world of different animals, of birds and sea creatures, Adam did not have a suitable companion. So God declared He would make a **helper** suitable for him. Notice the word, **"helper."**

Gen 2:20-21

But for Adam no suitable helper was found.

God therefore made woman, but He did so differently than he had all other living beings up to that point. Up to that point, every living thing had been created from the ground (soil) of the earth. Genesis 2:21–23 tells us this part of the story.

Gen 2:21–23

21 So the Lord God caused the man to fall into a deep sleep; and while he was sleeping, he took one of the man's ribs and closed up the place with flesh. 22 Then the Lord God made

a woman from the rib he had taken out of the man, and he brought her to the man.

23 The man said,

"This is now bone of my bones

and flesh of my flesh;

she shall be called 'woman,' for she was taken out of man."

Notice that woman was **not** made from the ground (soil) of the earth, but was made from the man! This made woman unique among all of creation. And also notice that when God made woman from the body of the man, He did not make her from the head of Adam, as though to be the head of Adam; nor did He make her from the foot of Adam, as though she was made to be tread upon; but no, He made her from the side of Adam, from one of his ribs, that she might walk alongside him, that they might be equals. And what was God thinking when He made woman by creating Eve? Genesis 2:24 gives us the answer.

Gen 2:24

24 For this reason a man will leave his father and mother and be united to his wife, and they will become one flesh.

Because God made woman **from** man and made her to be a **helper**, God intended that man would leave his father and mother and, becoming married, the man and the woman would become one. This tells us that you can't choose your mother or your father, but you can choose your wife. God's intent is that you will then become one. One in every way that she might become your suitable helper. God intends that this oneness includes all of what makes us human beings, what sets us apart from the entire rest of the created realm. And what does this oneness include? It includes emotionally, physically, spiritually, and intellectually! How do we know that? Because God revealed through His son, Jesus, what love looks like from God's perspective. Jesus shared this insight in Mark 12:30.

Mark 12:29–30

'Hear, O Israel, the Lord our God, the Lord is one. 30 Love the Lord your God with all your heart and with all your soul and with all your mind and with all your strength.'

So to further enlighten, Jesus is saying that to truly love and be one, we will love with our heart—which is our emotional center; with our soul—which is our spiritual center; with our mind—which is our intellectual center; and our strength—which is our physical center. There you have it! If we are to truly love and seek to be one, as God the Father, Son, and Holy Spirit are one, we will need to love our mates emotionally, spiritually, intellectually, and physically. How are you doing at this? If any one of these elements is missing from your relationship, you have a compromised relationship that cannot lead to the oneness that God intends. Ephesians 5:2 says it this way:

Eph 5:2, NLT

2 Live a life filled with love, following the example of Christ. He loved us and offered himself as a sacrifice for us, a pleasing aroma to God.

So true love, as modeled by Christ, has all four elements present in the relationship. Do you understand and grasp how important all four are to your success as a married couple?

Well, back to Genesis with a new question. **Why** create marriage? In fact, let us look at the age-old five W's of classic understanding applied to any story: Who, What, Where, Why, and When?

- Who created marriage? God did, as we have previously discussed.

- What is the purpose of marriage? To provide a foundation upon which a family can be formed which will enable mankind to accomplish what God had instructed; to be fruitful, multiply (not possible in a homosexual relationship), fill, subdue, and rule.
- Where was marriage created? In the mind of God and the rest of the trinity, and brought forth on the earth in the Garden of Eden.
- When was marriage created? Marriage was created when the first man and woman of humanity were on the earth, in the Garden of Eden.
- Why? Why was marriage created? Well, there are several reasons scripture gives us to understand the motive behind God creating marriage. The most straightforward of the reasons God tells us in **Malachi 2:14-15.**

15 Has not [the Lord] made them one? In flesh and spirit they are his. And why one? <u>Because he was seeking godly offspring.</u> So guard yourself in your spirit, and do not break faith with the wife of your youth.

Why? Again, to understand God's heart and mind, we have to look at scripture some more. To understand the "**why**" of marriage, we have to first understand the "**why**" of mankind in general. Fortunately, the Bible answers our question. Some of the scripture that points to and defines the answer is found in:

Deut 10:12-13

12 And now, O Israel, what does the Lord your God ask of you but to fear the Lord your God, to walk in all his ways, to love him, to serve the Lord your God with all your heart and

with all your soul, 13 and to observe the Lord's commands and decrees that I am giving you today for your own good?

Rev 14:7

7 He said in a loud voice, "Fear God and give him glory, because the hour of his judgment has come. Worship him who made the heavens, the earth, the sea and the springs of water."

Eccl 12:13–14

13 Now all has been heard;
here is the conclusion of the matter:
Fear God and keep his commandments,
for this is the whole [duty] of man.
14 For God will bring every deed into judgment,
including every hidden thing,
whether it is good or evil.

Ps 111:10

10 The fear of the Lord is the beginning of wisdom;
all who follow his precepts have good understanding.
To him belongs eternal praise.

Rev 19:5–9

5 Then a voice came from the throne, saying:
"Praise our God,
all you his servants,
you who fear him,
both small and great!"

6 Then I heard what sounded like a great multitude, like the
roar of rushing waters and like loud peals of thunder, shouting:
"Hallelujah!
For our Lord God Almighty reigns.

7 Let us rejoice and be glad
and give him glory!
For the wedding of the Lamb has come,
and his bride has made herself ready.

8 Fine linen, bright and clean,
was given her to wear."
(Fine linen stands for the righteous acts of the saints.)

9 Then the angel said to me, "Write: 'Blessed are those who are
invited to the wedding supper of the Lamb!'" And he added,
"These are the true words of God."

So, what do these scriptures tell us? That we were created to bring
praise, honor, and obedience to God. If that is the stated objective for
mankind in general, how does marriage fit into that purpose? Marriage
is symbolic of our being born into a family, not of our choosing, and in
this case born into the family of Satan. Satan is the God of the earth, and
until we reject the family of Satan and turn to our true love of **choice**, and
leave and cleave … until then, Satan is our father. By leaving and cleaving

to Christ, we can live in a love relationship of our choosing…and Christ, through the Holy Spirit, will be there to be our helpmate!

* Marriage and family provides the forum for God to teach us in a visible, tangible world, about the spiritual relationships He has also created. Hence…

* We can understand our roles as children and see the immaturity and foolishness that can translate to our spiritual walk discerned through our physical world both as we experience being a child, but also experience being a parent of a child or grandchild. The spiritual application becomes clearer as we gain more wisdom with respect to this physical world.

* We can understand our role as parents in the physical world and thereby understand the discipline, mercy, and grace of our Heavenly Father!

* We can understand what it means to have and to be "family." To understand what it means to be a brother or a sister in faith as joint heir with Jesus!

* All of the relationships that are established through human marriage and family and children mirror the spiritual relationships that God wants us to understand about His world while we are still in our world.

* Now, back to our original premise. We have just answered why God created marriage, so let us ask further,

* Why did God create woman? As a party to the marriage, with the purposes and goals we have just discussed, how does woman fit into those purposes and goals? What did we read earlier? That God could not find a helper suitable for Adam, so He made one from his side. So I ask again, what was God's intent? Answer: That women would help men achieve their full potential of worshipping, praising, and serving the God who made him. We are to serve Him through our work and worship. Woman is there to help man fulfill his commission to fill the

earth, to be productive in work and in having children, and to rule and have dominion over the rest of creation. If that was the role of women ... what happened?!

The Fall! Adam and Eve failed each other and failed God. How so? Adam failed to provide spiritual leadership for his wife, and Eve was deceived and made a bad decision that would affect both her and her husband, and he failed to stop her. Woman (Eve) let man down, and instead of helping him succeed, she coerced him into failure! Hence, God pronounced judgment! And what was that judgment? To woman He decreed:

Gen. 3:16

"I will greatly increase your pains in childbearing;
with pain you will give birth to children.
Your desire will be for your husband,
and he will rule over you."

To man He decreed:
Gen 3:17–19

17 To Adam he said, "Because you listened to your wife and ate from the tree about which I commanded you, 'You must not eat of it,'
"Cursed is the ground because of you;
through painful toil you will eat of it
all the days of your life.
18 It will produce thorns and thistles for you,
and you will eat the plants of the field.
19 By the sweat of your brow
you will eat your food
until you return to the ground,
since from it you were taken;

**for dust you are
and to dust you will return."**

So let's examine this judgment. Since God dealt with the woman first in pronouncing his judgment, let us first examine the consequences to women who have followed since Eve. The number one aspect of this judgment you all understand if you have had children. God promised pain in childbirth. Was He true to His Word, ladies? The second part of the judgment is that you would have desire for your husband. Do you understand what God meant by this phrase? He was not talking about desire in the sense that you usually use this word today. He wasn't talking about sexual attraction or lustful desire or desire for fellowship and companionship. The word translated desire here is the same word also used in **Genesis 4:7.**

7 If you do what is right, will you not be accepted? But if you do not do what is right, sin is crouching at your door; it desires to have you, but you must master it."

Used in this context, it is more apparent that desire is meant to reveal that you will want to devour, control, possess, and destroy, just like the sin that is crouching at your door. If that is true, what implications does this have for women ... and for marriage?

Answer: Woman is no longer motivated to be a help-mate, but she desires to control, manipulate, master, and possess her husband, thereby creating conflict. Satan's world, all around you, reinforces this viewpoint, and ridicules the idea of a submissive and servant-minded wife.

The third part of the judgment is that your husband will rule over you.

Question: Where on the earth, in what country or nation or culture, do women rule? Historically, where have they ruled?

Answer: **Nowhere!**

Question: What nations of the world accord women equality with men?

Answer: Only Western cultures.

Question: So, what constitutes a Western culture?

Answer: A culture whose civil laws are based on a Judeo-Christian foundation.

In other words women had no rights before Christianity, and now the only nations in the world in which women are equal with men are nations with laws based on the Bible. If their laws are based on the prophet Muhammad, or Buddha, or one of many Hindu gods, or the stars or the planets or any other basis other than the Bible, women are uniformly ruled by men and generally have no rights, are viewed as property and present only for the pleasure of men. It took Jesus Christ to reorder the relationship of men and women. He and He alone is responsible for giving women a place of honor, respect, and protection. Why then do women's rights activists hate the Biblical idea of submission and reject Christianity, and ridicule women who see themselves through the eyes of the Bible? It is because they are deceived by their father, the Father of Lies himself, Satan; just as Eve was deceived by him 6,000 years ago in the Garden of Eden.

Since God's choice was for you women to be a helper and helpmate to your husbands, how do you get back to His intended purpose for your life? Answer: You have to first learn to submit to Christ.

Eph 5:22–24

22 Wives, submit to your husbands as to the Lord. 23 For the husband is the head of the wife as Christ is the head of the church, his body, of which he is the Savior. 24 Now as the church submits to Christ, so also wives should submit to their husbands in everything.

God, in His goodness, explains this concept of submission as He shows us in the Bible how even in the trinity there is submission and a recognized hierarchy of authority. The Holy Spirit came to the earth at the request of Jesus Christ, and Jesus Christ came to the world at the request of the Father. Both were submitted to a higher authority.

John 14:23–31

23 Jesus replied, "If anyone loves me, he will obey my teaching. My Father will love him, and we will come to him and make our home with him. 24 He who does not love me will not obey my teaching. These words you hear are not my own; they belong to the Father who sent me.

25 "All this I have spoken while still with you. 26 But the Counselor, the Holy Spirit, whom the Father will send in my name, will teach you all things and will remind you of everything I have said to you. 27 Peace I leave with you; my peace I give you. I do not give to you as the world gives. Do not let your hearts be troubled and do not be afraid.

28 "You heard me say, 'I am going away and I am coming back to you.' If you loved me, you would be glad that I am going to the Father, for the Father is greater than I. 29 I have told you now before it happens, so that when it does happen you will believe. 30 I will not speak with you much longer, for the prince of this world is coming. He has no hold on me, 31 but the world must learn that I love the Father and that I do exactly what my Father has commanded me.

John 5:19–20

19 Jesus gave them this answer: "I tell you the truth, the Son can do nothing by himself; he can do only what he sees his Father doing, because whatever the Father does the Son also does.

John 5:30

30 By myself I can do nothing; I judge only as I hear, and my judgment is just, for I seek not to please myself but him who sent me.

John 12:49–50

49 For I did not speak of my own accord, but the Father who sent me commanded me what to say and how to say it. 50 I know that his command leads to eternal life. So whatever I say is just what the Father has told me to say."

Matt 24:36–37

36 "No one knows about that day or hour, not even the angels in heaven, nor the Son, but only the Father.

Ladies, what do you learn from these scriptures? It should be that there is ample Biblical support for the idea that submission is not a four-letter word and not something to resist, but is instead a part of the structure and organization of heaven and earth. The authority hierarchy as presented in the Bible is therefore God the Father, Jesus Christ the Son, the Holy Spirit, man, woman, children, then border collies, then the rest can fight it out! Ha! Women or wives must learn to submit to Christ, then their husbands, in order to fulfill the purpose God made them for and to receive the blessings He intended for you to enjoy... way back in the Garden of Eden! To be totally submitted means you no longer compete for control and manipulative dominance, but instead your total purpose is to help your husband achieve the full potential of what he can be *only* when he has you to complement his weaknesses and inadequacies.

Question: What are his weaknesses and inadequacies?
Answer: 1) difficulty in communicating
           2) difficulty in achieving order and balance
           3) difficulty in aligning priorities
           4) difficulty in dealing with failure and rejection
           5) difficulty in achieving contentment, peace, and joy
Question: How can you affect him for the good?
Answer: **Be** what he can't! **Do** what he can't! **Guide, encourage, and cheerlead!**

What form does this take?

CHAPTER TWO

Well, to understand how you can best help your husband, you have to have some understanding of the needs of a man as compared to the needs of a woman. When women look at men through their own eyes, they see folly, ego, bullying, and irrational pursuits. Why? Because they see men through the prism of their own needs and likes and dislikes ... not from his perspective! So if we are to truly understand our respective roles, we must of necessity understand what makes each other tick!

To arrive at this understanding, we have to understand how women and men perceive their needs in marriage. What are the needs that men typically identify? What are the needs that women typically identify? Well, thankfully, a clinical psychologist named Willard F. Harley, Jr. PhD, has studied this problem and written several books on the subject. His book, *His Needs, Her Needs*, catalogued the needs in marriages and found that when thousands of people were queried on the subject, there were ten common needs that both males and females identified as needs in their life. The list of ten things turned out to be the same list. The surprising fact to come from the research, however, was that when you ask men to rank order their needs from most important to least important and you asked women to do the same thing, the rank order for women was essentially the reverse order for a man! In other words, what was number one most important need for a man was number ten for a woman. And what was number one most important need for a woman was number ten for a man! Do you see the potential for conflict here? If you don't, you probably should not consider being married. Ha! Seriously! How much more opposite can you be? And we wonder why marriage is difficult?! Let me just state for the record ... **It is rigged!**

Yes, and the author of marriage rigged it intentionally! Why on earth would God intentionally create a rigged institution where there is guaranteed to be conflict? I have honestly already shared the answer with you, but let's review. God created marriage to give us insight into the spiritual world. If we are to understand the spiritual world, we have to understand the authority hierarchy and we have to understand the true meaning of love, in its four elements, and we have to understand how love is lived out in life on earth as well as life in heaven. To truly understand love, real love in all of its beauty and glory and sacrifice, we have to look to Jesus Christ who alone embodies all that it means to be love. John, the disciple of Jesus, wrote to us of that love. A sampling of the many passages that John wrote include:

1 John 2:3–6

3 We know that we have come to know him if we obey his commands. 4 The man who says, "I know him," but does not do what he commands is a liar, and the truth is not in him. 5 But if anyone obeys his word, God's love is truly made complete in him. This is how we know we are in him: 6 Whoever claims to live in him must walk as Jesus did.

---

1 John 2:15–17

15 Do not love the world or anything in the world. If anyone loves the world, the love of the Father is not in him. 16 For everything in the world — the cravings of sinful man, the lust of

his eyes and the boasting of what he has and does — comes not from the Father but from the world. 17 The world and its desires pass away, but the man who does the will of God lives forever.

---

1 John 3:16–20

This is how we know what love is: Jesus Christ laid down his life for us. And we ought to lay down our lives for our brothers. 17 If anyone has material possessions and sees his brother in need but has no pity on him, how can the love of God be in him? 18 Dear children, let us not love with words or tongue but with actions and in truth. 19 This then is how we know that we belong to the truth, and how we set our hearts at rest in his presence 20 whenever our hearts condemn us. For God is greater than our hearts, and he knows everything.

---

1 John 3:23–24

23 And this is his command: to believe in the name of his Son, Jesus Christ, and to love one another as he commanded us. 24 Those who obey his commands live in him, and he in them. And this is how we know that he lives in us: We know it by the Spirit he gave us.

1 John 4:8–12

8 Whoever does not love does not know God, because God is love. 9 This is how God showed his love among us: He sent his one and only Son into the world that we might live through him. 10 This is love: not that we loved God, but that he loved

us and sent his Son as an atoning sacrifice for our sins. 11 Dear friends, since God so loved us, we also ought to love one another. 12 No one has ever seen God; but if we love one another, God lives in us and his love is made complete in us.

---

1 John 4:16–21

God is love. Whoever lives in love lives in God, and God in him. 17 In this way, love is made complete among us so that we will have confidence on the day of judgment, because in this world we are like him. 18 There is no fear in love. But perfect love drives out fear, because fear has to do with punishment. The one who fears is not made perfect in love.
19 We love because he first loved us. 20 If anyone says, "I love God," yet hates his brother, he is a liar. For anyone who does not love his brother, whom he has seen, cannot love God, whom he has not seen. 21 And he has given us this command: Whoever loves God must also love his brother.

---

1 John 5:3–5

3 This is love for God: to obey his commands. And his commands are not burdensome, 4 for everyone born of God overcomes the world. This is the victory that has overcome the world, even our faith. 5 Who is it that overcomes the world? Only he who believes that Jesus is the Son of God.

So Jesus showed us what true love really is. When you distill the life of Jesus and His love down to its very essence, you understand that **true love has two characteristics**.

* 1) It is **self-sacrificing**, and
* 2) it is **self-disciplined**.

Jesus embodies these two characteristics. He demonstrated his love for us in that He left the throne room of heaven to become a baby on earth and endure abuse, anger, and injury at the hands of those He came to save … all because He loved us and was unwilling that any should perish, but that whosoever will may come and know eternal life. That, friends, is self-sacrifice in the highest order! Then he was self-disciplined when over and over he resisted the temptations that are common to all men, and yet He remained without sin. He was even personally tempted by Satan and yet had the discipline to simply quote scripture as His defense. He was committed to doing the will of the Father and His Will only. How much greater love has any man seen than the love of the Father and the Son for the lost souls of earth.

So how does all of this relate back to marriage and to maximizing your marriage? It is to understand that the role model for how to love is Jesus Christ who showed us that to truly love we need to manifest **self-sacrifice** and **self-discipline**! So when you assess your marriage and your role in your marriage … is it marked by the presence of self-sacrifice for your mate, whom you say you love…? Is it marked by self-discipline toward the mate you say you love? Or as John stated in the scripture we just read, are you a liar and the truth is not in you when you refuse to love a mate who is right there in front of you? Love in the way that Christ expects, not love as the world would tell you? If you want to really love as Christ expects you to love, He needs to challenge you to learn to love with **self-sacrifice** and **self-discipline**, and what better way to do that than to put you with another human being who has exactly the opposite needs as yours! If you are to truly experience love and begin to have a glimpse of the glory of heavenly love, you will need to approach your mate with the love that Christ came to show you when He loved you in your sin and rebellion.

That leads us back to understanding the needs of a man and the needs of a woman.

I mentioned earlier that there are three primary reasons why most couples divorce, namely **money**, **sex**, and **communication.** These three are actually a consolidation of the ten primary needs of men and women in marriage. Let's see if we can come up with a list of all ten. In no particular order, they are:

1) Affection
2) Sexual fulfillment
3) Conversation
4) Recreational companionship
5) Honesty and openness
6) Physical attractiveness
7) Financial support
8) Domestic support
9) Family commitment
10) Admiration

I would encourage you to write these down and then go home and consider how you would rank order these needs. How about your spouse? How different is the order between the two of you? Are you surprised at how different you are? Do you see a basis for conflict?

When we look at these ten areas of identified needs in the life of men and women, and we see how very different the priority order is between men and women, some questions start to form in our minds, such as:

* **Why** are men and women so different?
* In **what** ways are men and women different?
* How are we supposed to "become one" **when** we are so different?
* **Who** is able to succeed in becoming one?
* **Where** do we start to creating oneness?

As I just mentioned, the three primary causes of failed marriages are really just a consolidation of the ten basic needs of a man and a woman. Again, they are **money**, **sex**, and **communication**.

Money - ties back to financial support, domestic support, recreational companionship, and family commitment (of both time and money)

Sex - ties back to affection, sexual fulfillment, and physical attractiveness, and

Communication - relates to conversation, honesty and openness, and admiration.

We will work with the three big categories of challenge for marriages by looking at all three in some detail. Once we have developed a Biblical view for these three categories, the method and approach in addressing each of the ten more specific areas should be more apparent. From our earliest memories of life, we identify ourselves primarily as male or female. We recognize from earliest childhood that there is clearly a difference between boys and girls, despite the unending efforts of the progressive left in our culture who are trying to destroy the notion of gender and blur any lines between males and females. We all inherently know that our sex, our gender, has a great deal of effect on our view of the world. Since sex is so visible and pervasive in our culture, let's first look at sex as an area of opportunity to become more one in our marriage relationships. To properly address sex from a Biblical point of view, we have to ask whether the Bible has anything to say about sex and any recommendations to make as to how to manage this potent force in our lives. The answer is a resounding "Yes!" So let's look at sex from a biological, physiological, psychological, and spiritual perspective. God has given us one answer to a common question that society has asked for the past several millennia. **Did God create sex simply for pro-creation, or did He really intend it to be a source of pleasure?** In other words, is it wrong to seek or desire pleasure from sexual activity?

Well, God gave us a biological, anatomic answer to this question. He made woman with clitoris. What is the clitoris? What function does the clitoris have? Its only function is pleasure! It is a gland situated at the top of the vaginal opening that provides pleasure to a woman when touched and stimulated. Since God already pronounced that the woman He made was not just good but very good, it would seem obvious that God put the clitoris there because He fully intended and expected men and women to derive pleasure from sexual activity. More questions remain, however.

* Question #1: What are the differences in how males and females approach sex?

MALES	FEMALES
* greatly influenced by the saturation of sex in our culture in every aspect of life.	* interest is piqued as well in the dark
* interest generated immediately and unaffected by all but a few factors.	* emotional stimulation from movie, romance novel, or other similar stimuli
* build to orgasm quickly and quickly resolve.	* interest slow to develop and affected by many other factors
* usually long latency time to recovery before being ready for further sexual activity	* builds to orgasm slowly, tends to resolve slowly
* primarily focused on the end result, i.e., orgasm and ejaculation	* can experience multiple orgasms
	* very self-conscious about body image
	* mood affects interest, and mood may be secondary to activities or actions at a time somewhat distant to the moment.

    * there is no consistent stimulus
or combination of stimuli
that will lead to interest and
response.

You can clearly acknowledge from the differences described that **men and women are very different** in their approach to sex. To take the differences a step further, let us ask another question.

    * Question #2: What does sex do for a man? What does sex do for a woman?

To answer that, let us go back to the elements of love and think in terms of the physical, intellectual (mental), emotional, and spiritual dimensions to this relationship.

	MALES	FEMALES
Physical	provides peak of intensity followed by complete relaxation and stress dissipation	do not always reach orgasmic peak, and most do not need orgasm or expect orgasm or require orgasm every time to be satisfied.
Intellectual/ Mental	provides affirmation that spouse is responsive and submissive	affirmation of commitment to relationship
Emotional	provides a "safe" garden to relax and de-stress provides inoculation against insults, stress, and demands of life.	affirmation of appeal, of being desired, sought after being pursued ... i.e., romance
Spiritual	An intimacy that bonds two people together, as a part of yourself is given to another	the same response in a woman as in a man
PEARL	Men give romance to get sex	Women give sex to get romance

That brings us to yet another question.

* Question #3: **Why** are men/women so different? (They obviously are!)

I believe that the answer to this question is that **God rigged it this way!** And why would He do that?! We have already established the premise that God desires Godly offspring, and that God intended that the two should become one. He also tells us in His Word that His primary desire is that we would become like His son! How is He going to help men and women become more like His son? By putting together two people who look at the world from two different points of view, two different sets of needs, two different responses to circumstances, two different goals, and forcing them to learn to work together to avoid conflict, stress, and tension in their relationship. And what characteristics is He trying to build into our lives? The qualities of **self-sacrifice** and **self-discipline!** What better way to achieve that goal than to throw these two people into life together where they are together for most meals, sleep together, are exposed to each other's flaws and failures, and provide the sandpaper of life that will rub the rough edges smooth and sand out the imperfections. In my mind, it is quite ingenious. And in so doing, He teaches us to give for the greater good, he teaches us not to demand our rights, he teaches us to persevere, He teaches us by having someone around to point out our shortcomings. And as a bonus, He reveals to us the relationship dynamics of heaven itself and how to be more like Jesus Christ who gave himself for the greater good, ignoring His rights to instead provide for the redemption of mankind who was rebellious, defiant, selfish, and prideful. We as men and women are so different because it is true that opposites attract. We are different because the differences in our spouses create interest, in addition to aggravation.

Moving on to our next question.

✳ Question #4: Why does God have such a narrow framework around sexual intercourse? And in fact, what is His framework for sexual activity?

Ex 20:14

14 "You shall not commit adultery.

_____

Ex 20:17

17 "You shall not covet your neighbor's house. You shall not covet your neighbor's wife, or his manservant or maidservant, his ox or donkey, or anything that belongs to your neighbor."

_____

Matt 5:27–29

27 "You have heard that it was said, 'Do not commit adultery.' 28 But I tell you that anyone who looks at a woman lustfully has already committed adultery with her in his heart.

_____

1 Cor 6:12–20

12 "Everything is permissible for me"-but not everything is beneficial. "Everything is permissible for me"-but I will not be mastered by anything. 13 "Food for the stomach and the stomach for food"-but God will destroy them both. The body is not meant for sexual immorality, but for the Lord, and the Lord for the body. 14 By his power God raised the Lord from the

dead, and he will raise us also. 15 Do you not know that your bodies are members of Christ himself? Shall I then take the members of Christ and unite them with a prostitute? Never! 16 Do you not know that he who unites himself with a prostitute is one with her in body? For it is said, "The two will become one flesh." 17 But he who unites himself with the Lord is one with him in spirit.

18 Flee from sexual immorality. All other sins a man commits are outside his body, but he who sins sexually sins against his own body. 19 Do you not know that your body is a temple of the Holy Spirit, who is in you, whom you have received from God? You are not your own; 20 you were bought at a price. Therefore honor God with your body.

Heb 13:4–5

Marriage should be honored by all, and the marriage bed kept pure, for God will judge the adulterer and all the sexually immoral.

---

1 Cor 5:11

11 But now I am writing you that you must not associate with anyone who calls himself a brother but is sexually immoral

1 Cor 5:11

With such a man do not even eat.

Col 3:5

5 Put to death, therefore, whatever belongs to your earthly
nature: sexual immorality,

Rom 1:18–32

18 The wrath of God is being revealed from heaven against all
the godlessness and wickedness of men who suppress the truth
by their wickedness, 19 since what may be known about God
is plain to them, because God has made it plain to them. 20
For since the creation of the world God's invisible qualities—
his eternal power and divine nature—have been clearly seen,
being understood from what has been made, so that men are
without excuse.
21 For although they knew God, they neither glorified him as
God nor gave thanks to him, but their thinking became futile
and their foolish hearts were darkened. 22 Although they
claimed to be wise, they became fools 23 and exchanged the
glory of the immortal God for images made to look like mor-
tal man and birds and animals and reptiles.
24 Therefore God gave them over in the sinful desires of their
hearts to sexual impurity for the degrading of their bodies
with one another. 25 They exchanged the truth of God for a
lie, and worshiped and served created things rather than the
Creator—who is forever praised. Amen.
26 Because of this, God gave them over to shameful lusts. Even
their women exchanged natural relations for unnatural ones.
27 In the same way the men also abandoned natural relations
with women and were inflamed with lust for one another.

Men committed indecent acts with other men, and received in themselves the due penalty for their perversion.

28 Furthermore, since they did not think it worthwhile to retain the knowledge of God, he gave them over to a depraved mind, to do what ought not to be done. 29 They have become filled with every kind of wickedness, evil, greed and depravity. They are full of envy, murder, strife, deceit and malice. They are gossips, 30 slanderers, God-haters, insolent, arrogant and boastful; they invent ways of doing evil; they disobey their parents; 31 they are senseless, faithless, heartless, ruthless. 32 Although they know God's righteous decree that those who do such things deserve death, they not only continue to do these very things but also approve of those who practice them.

Lev 18:22-29

22 "Do not lie with a man as one lies with a woman; that is detestable.

23 "Do not have sexual relations with an animal and defile yourself with it. A woman must not present herself to an animal to have sexual relations with it; that is a perversion.

24 "Do not defile yourselves in any of these ways, because this is how the nations that I am going to drive out before you became defiled. 25 Even the land was defiled; so I punished it for its sin, and the land vomited out its inhabitants. 26 But you must keep my decrees and my laws. The native-born and the aliens living among you must not do any of these detestable things, 27 for all these things were done by the people who lived in the land before you, and the land became defiled. 28

And if you defile the land, it will vomit you out as it vomited out the nations that were before you.

Lev 20:13

13 "'If a man lies with a man as one lies with a woman, both of them have done what is detestable. They must be put to death; their blood will be on their own heads.

Deut 23:17–18

17 No Israelite man or woman is to become a shrine prostitute. 18 You must not bring the earnings of a female prostitute or of a male prostitute into the house of the Lord your God to pay any vow, because the Lord your God detests them both.

---

1 Cor 6:9–11

9 Do you not know that the wicked will not inherit the kingdom of God? Do not be deceived: Neither the sexually immoral nor idolaters nor adulterers nor male prostitutes nor homosexual offenders 10 nor thieves nor the greedy nor drunkards nor slanderers nor swindlers will inherit the kingdom of God. 11 And that is what some of you were. But you were washed, you were sanctified, you were justified in the name of the Lord Jesus Christ and by the Spirit of our God.

Eph 4:19

19 Having lost all sensitivity, they have given themselves over to sensuality so as to indulge in every kind of impurity, with a continual lust for more.

God has a narrow framework around sexual activity, because just as we read from His Word, He is going to punish people who pursue sex outside of marriage, and because as His Word just told us, we will incur a penalty in our bodies from disobedience to God's Word. Said another way, God has restricted sexual activity to just between a husband and a wife, because **He was trying to protect men and women from the physical, emotional, mental and spiritual consequences of disobeying His Word**. He did it for our own good!

*   Question #5: What scriptures talk about sex?

Song of Solomon - The entire book! All eight chapters, but particularly chapter 4:1 to 5:1.

---

1 Cor 7:1-9

7 Now for the matters you wrote about: It is good for a man not to marry. 2 But since there is so much immorality, each man should have his own wife, and each woman her own husband. 3 The husband should fulfill his marital duty to his wife, and likewise the wife to her husband. 4 The wife's body does not belong to her alone but also to her husband. In the same way, the husband's body does not belong to him alone but also to his wife. 5 Do not deprive each other except by mutual consent and for a time, so that you may devote yourselves to prayer.

Then come together again so that Satan will not tempt you because of your lack of self-control. 6 I say this as a concession, not as a command. 7 I wish that all men were as I am. But each man has his own gift from God; one has this gift, another has that. 8 Now to the unmarried and the widows I say: It is good for them to stay unmarried, as I am. 9 But if they cannot control themselves, they should marry, for it is better to marry than to burn with passion.

Paul has addressed in 1 Corinthians the primary motive for men to get married. What is it that he acknowledged? It is that males are so tempted to pursue sexual immorality that they should get married so that their sexual needs can be met. He mentions women in the same verse, and while women also enjoy and seek sexual activity, it is clear in any study of men and women that men are much more consumed with meeting their sexual needs. So if we are to follow Paul's admonition with respect to this powerful drive, what is his revelation to married couples regarding sex? It is first to acknowledge that we have a **"duty"** to each other to provide our spouse sexual satisfaction. He further describes a principle in marriage, and that is that once married, the wife's body is not hers alone, to do with only as she desires, nor is the husband's body his alone but belongs to his wife as well. What is this intended to convey? Isn't it pretty plain? The principle that he is describing (which can be applied to all ten needs in marriage) is that we give up individual rights when we get married, and they get merged together so that our spouse has a claim on even our body! This is certainly counterculture, is it not?! Why do you think Paul describes this with respect to sex? The answer is that Paul recognized that since a man has such tremendous, God-given drive to seek sexual fulfillment, his fulfillment could only come from his wife if he is to live according to the plan of God. That means that if he is monogamous with his wife, then the only avenue for a man to achieve fulfillment of his most pressing need after air, water and food, is that he has to rely on his wife to meet that need. It can't be predicated on when she is in the mood, or dependent on how the kids were today or whether she is tired, or that she is just feeling cranky today. No, Paul is saying to women that you have a **duty**, and your husband has a **right**, to have his sexual needs fulfilled by you according to **his** needs, *not* yours!

If you are the exception to the rule and you, as a wife, have a stronger sex drive than your husband, then you also deserve to have him provide you with sexual activity sufficient to meet **your** needs. While sex may be the primary topic here, the principle is just as important to the whole of the marriage relationship in areas having nothing to do with sex. The biggest difference between the sexual needs and the other nine needs is that most of the other needs can be met by other people, other organizations, by children, grandchildren, or activities by oneself. The sexual need stands alone in the fact that to be moral and righteous, the only person on the entire planet who can meet your sexual needs is your spouse. And to be even more pointed, men in their need for sexual gratification need more than just orgasm. Wives can communicate their disdain for sexual activity by phrases like, "If you have to go ahead, but hurry!" That is a good way to wound and cripple your mate, to essentially castrate him and make him feel devalued and rejected. You add to the devaluing of his sharing the most intimate aspect of his being with you when you refuse to participate in sexual activity in a way that is meaningful to him, and instead of sharing your body with him and focusing on being his delight, you expose just enough to "get it over with." While you may have fulfilled the letter of the law by consenting to intercourse, you have wounded your mate and created pain. Pain creates anger, and anger creates lack of emotional intimacy, which leads to lowered commitment, which leads to substitution from anyone who can stop the pain. Hence, affairs develop, and pornography gets a foothold.

You ladies have that power…and honestly…you have not used it very well. You have not used it as God intended. You have far too often used sex as a bargaining chip—implied or stated. You have wrangled "tit for tat"—both literally and figuratively. So, since we're picking on you ladies (men, your turn is coming!) what else can you do to be his helpmate?

* Be his sounding board!
* Help him think through options, choices, and decisions ... but ... be eager to relinquish the final decision *and* the final outcome to him.
* Support him, even in failure!
* Be his biggest cheerleader, **not** his biggest critic!
* What scripture supports these recommendations?

Eph 5:21–5:33, NLT

21 And further, submit to one another out of reverence for Christ.

22 For wives, this means submit your husbands as to the Lord.

23 For a husband is the head of his wife as Christ is the head of the church. He is the Savior of his body, the church.

24 As the church submits to Christ, so you wives should submit to your husbands in everything.

25 For husbands, this means love your wives, just as Christ loved the church. He gave up his life for her

26 to make her holy and clean, washed by the cleansing of God's word.

27 He did this to present her to himself as a glorious church without a spot or wrinkle or any other blemish. Instead, she will be holy and without fault.

28 In the same way, husbands ought to love their wives as they love their own bodies. For a man who loves his wife actually shows love for himself.

29 No one hates his own body but feeds and cares for it, just as Christ cares for the church.

30 And we are members of his body.

31 As the Scriptures say, "A man leaves his father and mother and is joined to his wife, and the two are united into one."

32 This is a great mystery, but it is an illustration of the way Christ and the church are one.

33 So again I say, each man must love his wife as he loves himself, and the wife must respect her husband.

Col 3:12–4:1

12 Therefore, as God's chosen people, holy and dearly loved, clothe yourselves with compassion, kindness, humility, gentleness and patience. 13 Bear with each other and forgive whatever grievances you may have against one another. Forgive as the Lord forgave you. 14 And over all these virtues put on love, which binds them all together in perfect unity.

15 Let the peace of Christ rule in your hearts, since as members of one body you were called to peace. And be thankful. 16 Let the word of Christ dwell in you richly as you teach and admonish one another with all wisdom, and as you sing psalms, hymns and spiritual songs with gratitude in your hearts to God. 17 And whatever you do, whether in word or deed, do it all in the name of the Lord Jesus, giving thanks to God the Father through him.

18 Wives, submit to your husbands, as is fitting in the Lord.

19 Husbands, love your wives and do not be harsh with them.

20 Children, obey your parents in everything, for this pleases the Lord.

21 Fathers, do not embitter your children, or they will become discouraged.

22 Slaves, obey your earthly masters in everything; and do it,

not only when their eye is on you and to win their favor, but with sincerity of heart and reverence for the Lord.

23 Whatever you do, work at it with all your heart, as working for the Lord, not for men,

24 since you know that you will receive an inheritance from the Lord as a reward. It is the Lord Christ you are serving.

25 Anyone who does wrong will be repaid for his wrong, and there is no favoritism.

Col 3:12–4:1

1 Masters, provide your slaves with what is right and fair, because you know that you also have a Master in heaven.

When we look at these scriptures, we see many lessons for marriage. If we study each verse, we will pick up some topics to explore. The first is the emphasis placed on submission. We have already talked about that term in this series, but by way of review, let us remind ourselves that submission is only a recognition of the chain of authority that God has established. It in no way relates to worth, value, or importance—it is simply the reflection of the order that God has built into the world. God -> Jesus Christ -> Holy Spirit -> man -> woman. This order is mirrored in the hierarchy in the church, as seen in

Eph 4:11–13, NLT

11 Now these are the gifts Christ gave to the church: the apostles, the prophets, the evangelists, and the pastors and teachers. 12 Their responsibility is to equip God's people to do his work and build up the church, the body of Christ. 13 This will continue until we all come to such unity in our faith and

knowledge of God's Son that we will be mature in the Lord, measuring up to the full and complete standard of Christ.

The point is that God has created a hierarchy in heaven, on earth, and even in the church. The twenty-second and the twenty-fourth verses in Ephesians 5 emphasize **submission in everything**. Everything?! **Yes! Everything!** In verse 25 we are told that we are to submit and love just like Christ did the church.

Question: How did Christ love the church?

He *gave* His life for the church; He *gave* her the gift of the Holy Spirit; He *gave* her His power and presence, and promises of provision and protection!

Some of His promises are:

Matt 28:20

20 and teaching them to obey everything I have commanded you. And surely I am with you always, to the very end of the age."

Matt 11:28–30

28 "Come to me, all you who are weary and burdened, and I will give you rest. 29 Take my yoke upon you and learn from me, for I am gentle and humble in heart, and you will find rest for your souls. 30 For my yoke is easy and my burden is light."

John 14:1–4

14 "Do not let your hearts be troubled. Trust in God; trust also in me. 2 In my Father's house are many rooms; if it were not so,

I would have told you. I am going there to prepare a place for you. 3 And if I go and prepare a place for you, I will come back and take you to be with me that you also may be where I am.

Jesus' prayer in John 17 also reiterates the concept that Jesus has done all He has done for the sake of the Father; that Jesus wants those who follow Him to see the glory that the Father gave to Jesus from eternity past, and that Jesus wants his followers to become one, even as Jesus and the Father are one. This kind of love is the kind of love that husbands are expected to give to their wives. It is a self-sacrificing love. It is a love that is like the love a man has for his own body. Every man takes care of his own body. He feeds it, cleans it, and nurses it when it is injured or sick. No one, no man, is oblivious to the needs of his own body. He seeks warmth when his body is cold, and food when his body is hungry. Paul, in the passage in Ephesians, directs men to love their wives in this same way. Husbands, that means that you will respond to the needs of your wife. You will be as good to her as you are to your own body! Paul even acknowledges that men who love their wives in this way are actually being good to themselves! How is this the case? It is a realization that when a woman is truly loved by her husband as he loves and cares for his own body, she will in turn be motivated to take care of him because she has no fear of being taken advantage of or being abused. The relationship becomes one of unity and "oneness." Paul ends this passage in Ephesians 5 by introducing a new word and thought into our understanding. It is the word "respect" used in verse 33.

He said that wives should "**respect**" their husbands. What is meant by the word "respect"? This word is not meant to convey that you wives are to respect your husbands just because he is the one you married, and now you are stuck with him. This is not a word that is meant to convey that you give him respect if he satisfactorily demonstrates a righteous, Christlike pattern of behavior of which you approve. No, what Paul is teaching here is that it is incumbent upon a wife to give respect to her husband because of the office he holds. First, let's define "respect." *Webster's New World*

Dictionary defines it as, "to feel or show honor or esteem for, to consider or treat with deference or courtesy." What Paul is saying is that because God placed your husband in the role of husband, and because God created the authority hierarchy of God the Father, God the Son, God the Holy Spirit, then man, then women, then children. It is because of the station or position that your husband holds that God expects you to show him honor, esteem, deference, and courtesy ... or otherwise ... respect! To put this in perspective, let me give you a more real-life example. When_____ (fill in the name of a president you didn't or don't like) was president of the United States (and thank God he is no longer!), I had no admiration or respect for him as a man, because my assessment was that he was a liar, a manipulator, and a typical, slick politician. I would not trust him in any personal dealing. I would have no interest in having a meal with him, or having him over to my home. **But** as president of the United States of America, if President_____ (again, your choice!) had invited me to the White House for a meal, or meeting or discussion, I would count it an honor and I would dress my best, and show him respect and honor and deference, not because I admire him as a man, but because I have so much respect and admiration for the office of the president of the United States, that whoever occupies that position and holds that office will elicit respect and honor from me. How does that relate to you wives and your husbands? Just like I did not agree with a previous president and his ideology, or his character qualities, I would show him respect not for what he has done or didn't do, but simply for the office he holds. Your husbands may or may not be a good husband, but God expects you to show him respect, not for what he has done or not done, but for the office that he holds. If his life merits even greater respect because he has lived a life of faithfulness, provision and protection, then God be praised! But even if he is a disappointment, you need to show him respect. This, too, is counterculture.

This acknowledgement of "position" or "office" is further seen in a passage by the apostle Peter.

1 Peter 2:13–3:1, NLT

13 For the Lord's sake, respect all human authority—whether the king as head of state, 14 or the officials he has appointed. For the king has sent them to punish those who do wrong and to honor those who do right.

15 It is God's will that your honorable lives should silence those ignorant people who make foolish accusations against you. 16 For you are free, yet you are God's slaves, so don't use your freedom as an excuse to do evil. 17 Respect everyone, and love your Christian brothers and sisters. Fear God, and respect the king.

Slaves

18 You who are slaves must accept the authority of your masters with all respect. Do what they tell you—not only if they are kind and reasonable, but even if they are cruel. 19 For God is pleased with you when you do what you know is right and patiently endure unfair treatment. 20 Of course, you get no credit for being patient if you are beaten for doing wrong. But if you suffer for doing good and endure it patiently, God is pleased with you.

21 For God called you to do good, even if it means suffering, just as Christ suffered for you. He is your example, and you must follow in his steps.

22 He never sinned,
nor ever deceived anyone.
23 He did not retaliate when he was insulted,
nor threaten revenge when he suffered.
He left his case in the hands of God,
who always judges fairly.
24 He personally carried our sins

in his body on the cross
so that we can be dead to sin
and live for what is right.
By his wounds
you are healed.
25 Once you were like sheep
who wandered away.
But now you have turned to your Shepherd,
the Guardian of your souls.

What Peter is commending here is the requirement to submit to authority, to those whom God has placed in even a civil position of authority. Notice the concept that we submit because of their office or position of authority, whether or not they are good or bad, or whether we like them or not. His position is that we need to keep the perspective that we are living for God and His expectations, not men. Peter then transitions to marriage, having just discussed yielding in submission to the authority hierarchy. We see this in

1 Peter 3:1–18, NLT

3 In the same way, you wives must accept the authority of your husbands. Then, even if some refuse to obey the Good News, your godly lives will speak to them without any words. They will be won over 2 by observing your pure and reverent lives.
3 Don't be concerned about the outward beauty of fancy hairstyles, expensive jewelry, or beautiful clothes. 4 You should clothe yourselves instead with the beauty that comes from within, the unfading beauty of a gentle and quiet spirit, which is so precious to God. 5 This is how the holy women of old made themselves beautiful. They trusted God and accepted the authority of their husbands. 6 For instance, Sarah obeyed her husband, Abraham, and called him her master. You are her

daughters when you do what is right without fear of what your husbands might do.

Husbands

7 In the same way, you husbands must give honor to your wives. Treat your wife with understanding as you live together. She may be weaker than you are, but she is your equal partner in God's gift of new life. Treat her as you should so your prayers will not be hindered.

All Christians

8 Finally, all of you should be of one mind. Sympathize with each other. Love each other as brothers and sisters. Be tender-hearted, and keep a humble attitude. 9 Don't repay evil for evil. Don't retaliate with insults when people insult you. Instead, pay them back with a blessing. That is what God has called you to do, and he will bless you for it. 10 For the Scriptures say,

"If you want to enjoy life
and see many happy days,
keep your tongue from speaking evil
and your lips from telling lies.
11 Turn away from evil and do good.
Search for peace, and work to maintain it.
12 The eyes of the Lord watch over those who do right,
and his ears are open to their prayers.
But the Lord turns his face
against those who do evil."

Suffering for Doing Good

13 Now, who will want to harm you if you are eager to do good? 14 But even if you suffer for doing what is right, God will reward you for it. So don't worry or be afraid of their threats. 15 Instead, you must worship Christ as Lord of your life. And if someone asks about your Christian hope, always be ready to explain it. 16 But do this in a gentle and respectful way. Keep your conscience clear. Then if people speak against you, they will be ashamed when they see what a good life you live because you belong to Christ. 17 Remember, it is better to suffer for doing good, if that is what God wants, than to suffer for doing wrong!

18 Christ suffered for our sins once for all time. He never sinned, but he died for sinners to bring you safely home to God. He suffered physical death, but he was raised to life in the Spirit.

Wow! There is a lot to unpack in that scripture passage! First, what is the lesson we are to learn from verse 1 and 2 that applies to marriage?

* It is that wives are to accept the authority of their husbands because of the office or position that they hold, not necessarily because of how good or bad a husband they are. What else do we learn that applies to marriage?

* That wives may win unbelieving husbands to the Lord when they live out their faith as Christ would have them live. That means that Christian wives do not treat their husbands as women in the world who don't know Christ would treat their husbands. The difference will be so significant and so unexplainable that it will provoke men to seek salvation! What a countercultural approach! Peter goes on to say that your true beauty as woman is not fine, expensive clothes, or jewelry or

hairstyles, but real beauty is because of a quiet and gentle spirit. He notes that God really values a woman with true beauty. He further notes that this is characterized by trusting God and being submissive to the authority of your husband. Then Peter ended this teaching toward wives by saying that you will be viewed as the holy women of the past if you do what is right without fear of what your husbands do. Another translation words it, "Give way to fear." What did Peter mean by that phrase? He meant that your natural temptation is to be fearful of the consequences of submitting to your husband, and so you reject submission and vie for control! (Remember the curse of Gen 4:16?!) Yes, 6,000 years later, after God cursed woman because of Eve's sin, you ladies still struggle with wanting to control, manipulate, and have mastery over your husbands. God views you as precious when you decide to live His way.

CHAPTER THREE

Having mentioned wives, let us stop for a minute and see what God has to say about wives. Does He have anything to say about wives? Yes, actually, God gives several insights into his view of a wife.

Prov 12:4

4 A wife of noble character is her husband's crown,
but a disgraceful wife is like decay in his bones.

Prov 14:1

14 The wise woman builds her house,
but with her own hands the foolish one tears hers down.

Prov 18:22

22 He who finds a wife finds what is good
and receives favor from the Lord.

Prov 19:14

14 Houses and wealth are inherited from parents,
but a prudent wife is from the Lord.

Prov 31:10–31

10 A wife of noble character who can find? She is worth far
more than rubies. 11 Her husband has full confidence in her
and lacks nothing of value. 12 She brings him good, not harm,
all the days of her life. 13 She selects wool and flax and works
with eager hands. 14 She is like the merchant ships, bringing
her food from afar. 15 She gets up while it is still dark; she provides food for her family and portions for her servant girls. 16
She considers a field and buys it; out of her earnings she plants
a vineyard. 17 She sets about her work vigorously; her arms
are strong for her tasks. 18 She sees that her trading is prof-
itable, and her lamp does not go out at night. 19 In her hand
she holds the distaff and grasps the spindle with her fingers. 20
She opens her arms to the poor and extends her hands to the
needy. 21 When it snows, she has no fear for her household;
for all of them are clothed in scarlet. 22 She makes coverings
for her bed; she is clothed in fine linen and purple. 23 Her
husband is respected at the city gate, where he takes his seat
among the elders of the land. 24 She makes linen garments and
sells them, and supplies the merchants with sashes. 25 She is
clothed with strength and dignity; she can laugh at the days
to come. 26 She speaks with wisdom, and faithful instruction
is on her tongue. 27 She watches over the affairs of her house
hold and does not eat the bread of idleness. 28 Her children
arise and call her blessed; her husband also, and he praises her:

**29 "Many women do noble things, but you surpass them all."
30 Charm is deceptive, and beauty is fleeting; but a woman
who fears the Lord is to be praised. 31 Give her the reward she
has earned, and let her works bring her praise at the city gate.**

So now Peter shifts to husbands, and he introduces this instruction by the phrase, "In the same way." He has also prefaced his remarks to wives with the same phrase. To what was he referring? He was looking back to the second chapter and his discussion of respecting those in positions of authority, and in stating the expectation that we husbands would live like Christ, even if we suffer for doing good. Peter instructs husbands to give honor to their wives. If we look at Webster's definition of "honor," we find by application that Peter is saying that we should give esteem, respect, deference, and even reverence to our wives because of who they are in God's eyes. God instructs us, through Peter, to treat our wives with understanding as we live together. The literal translation of this phrase is, "living together according to knowledge." What is Peter talking about? He is instructing men that they should study their wives and seek to obtain an understanding of their needs and wants, and fears and delights. He is acknowledging that left to his own inclinations, man would simply seek to impose his will on women because he is stronger physically. Peter is admonishing us men that contrary to our natural inclination, we need to study our wives purposefully. You can all surely recognize that women naturally study their husbands. They do this in part because they want to control us, and to do so they need to understand us, but it is also an acknowledgement of the differences between a man and a woman. Men, by and large, are not that complicated. They want to eat, have sex, and work. It doesn't take a lot of study of most men to figure out what their needs and likes and dislikes are. We men as a group are generally pretty transparent to anyone who will take the time to study us, even for a short time. Women, on the other hand, are much more complicated and complex. They don't even understand themselves or each other. What drives them one day may change the next day for reasons they neither understand nor their husbands can explain. But it doesn't mean that men should not try and understand their wives. It means that it takes a more deliberate and persistent study of your wife to really understand her and her fears, her needs and desires. It is incumbent upon husbands, if they are to be able to meet the needs of their wife, to endeavor to discern as much about their wife as they can. Only then can a husband truly serve his wife in a way that provides deep satisfaction and contentment without fear. Peter mentions that we are to treat her as the equal that God sees her as, despite the fact that she is physically weaker. The word used here is the word *asthenesteroo*, from which we derive the word "asthenia." We use this word in medicine when we describe "myasthenia gravis" in a patient with profound and "grave" muscle weakness. The best illustration I know to explain the thought behind Peter's statement is a plate analogy. Guys can go to the deer camp with metal plates that can be dropped and scrubbed with sand and heated over a fire, and stuffed in a duffle bag. It requires no gentle consideration to use this type of plate. It is tough and durable, and will stand up to abuse. This is analogous to a man. The woman can be compared to fine china or porcelain in this analogy. You clearly would not handle your great grandmother's fine china with the same carelessness of a deer camp plate. You would instead give it great care, consideration, and respect because you recognized that it is very fragile. Both plates are equally serviceable for eating, but they are handled very differently. Notice that Peter refers not only to women being weaker, but he calls them a partner! This is meant to signify equality! He clearly does not expect husbands to think of their wives as a servant, or "my old lady" or "the little woman," or "my bitch"! He is referencing the fact that God views women as having the same standing with God as men, just in a different role.

Gal 3:26–29

26 You are all sons of God through faith in Christ Jesus, 27 for all of you who were baptized into Christ have clothed yourselves with Christ. 28 There is neither Jew nor Greek, slave nor free, male nor female, for you are all one in Christ Jesus. 29 If you belong to Christ, then you are Abraham's seed, and heirs according to the promise.

And then Peter shares another truth with tremendous implications to husbands! He states that we need to treat our wives as we should so that our prayers are not hindered! Let's rephrase that in a more direct statement: If a man doesn't treat his wife as he should, his prayers will be hindered! Say what?! Yes, God is putting teeth into his expectations of how husbands should treat their wives by saying that he will not pay attention to you praying if you are not treating your wife properly. God also tells us in scripture that he protects the widow and the orphan. God is a protector of the weak! Women: as your protector, God will punish your husbands, so you don't need to try and take on that role. You submit and trust God. Let God provide the discipline! This is yet another example of the way that God rigs the system! He won't let men get by with using their strength to abuse women. So men, if your prayer life is ineffective and you don't feel like your prayers penetrate the ceiling, then this may be a place to start in restoring God's favor and listening ear. A further cautionary note: what this entire passage of Peter—and what we read from Paul in Ephesians and again in Colossians—is that God expects us husbands to seek to understand and meet the needs of our wives. They need us to listen to them, to discern their fears, needs and wants, and desires and dreams. And when you listen to them, don't mock and belittle them for their fears or feelings, even when it makes no sense to you. Women are not always objective and rational, and predicated on factual information, but at times are reacting from an emotional response that they can't even understand that may well just be a sixth sense and not correlated to anything you can quantify, measure, or assess objectively. But just as you do not want God mocking you for your fears, which are unfounded to Him, or your uncertainty, because you have not sought him, God wants you men to listen to your wives and be responsive to their needs whether you can understand or explain them or not. Peter then closed this extended passage in his gospel where he has talked about 1) friends, 2) slaves, 3) wives, and then 4) husbands by a final admonition in verses 8 and 9. That is:

* 1) live in harmony
* 2) be sympathetic
* 3) love as brothers
* 4) be compassionate
* 5) be humble
* 6) don't return insult for insult but with a blessing, and
* 7) give a blessing that you may receive a blessing.

Colossians 3:18 to 4:1 affirms the same instructions we have just completed, only in a different book of the Bible. There are not any new points to make from that parallel passage except that he adds the admonition to husbands that they should never treat their wives harshly. How many husbands can say that they have never treated their wives harshly? We have been given a standard to achieve, men.

CHAPTER FOUR

That brings us to a discussion of women, of wives and their needs. As we have previously discussed, although men's primary need is sex, it is rare that that is the primary need of women. Instead, when you look at how women describe and rank order their needs, one of their top needs is conversation. This falls under the banner of communication, which we have already stipulated is one of the top three reasons why couples divorce. This is equally as important to a woman as sex is to a man. Said even more directly, **"Conversation is to a woman what sex is to a man!"** Men are generally as dumbfounded that women put so much emphasis and priority on conversation as women are dumbfounded that men put so much emphasis and priority on sex! Both genders tend to think the other gender is warped or perverted to have such an irrational need! Well, just as we determined the principle behind how women should handle their responsiveness to the sexual needs of their husbands, we can apply the same principles to how men should respond to the conversation needs of their wives. In fact, the same principles apply to each of the ten primary needs of men and women in marriage. How God intended for husbands and wives to obtain fulfillment and satisfaction is through marriage. His plan was that they would both seek to serve the other, meet the needs of the other, and live in a manner consistent with how Jesus Christ loved the church and sinners in general. With respect to conversation, what is it that women need, and how do they achieve fulfillment?

First, it should be noted that women as a gender speak an average of 25,000 words per day. The average man speaks 5,000 words per day. Women love to talk! They are happy to create any excuse or activity that gives them a forum for conversation. They may ostensibly be together for a garden club, a cooking class, or a scrapbooking class, but the real delight for them is not in the cooking or the scrapbook, but in the conversation with other women. Their conversation is not focused and pertinent to the subject at hand, as is seen with men. Hence, the title of a book describing men and women, which is, **Men are waffles, women are spaghetti**. The thrust of the book is that men compartmentalize their life, and they tend to deal with life in discrete boxes of information and application. They deal with life one at a time, and do not wander from box to box. Also, whatever is in one box does not necessarily affect the other boxes. Women, on the other hand, are noted to be like spaghetti, in that they never follow a straight path, and they are always intersecting with another path and taking off on it. They manage many strands at a time, i.e., multitasking, but anything that affects one strand is likely to affect all the strands. An example of what I am talking about is that men can be in a meeting and have a very sharp disagreement, get somewhat heated in rebuttal of each other, but as soon as the meeting is over, they can move to the next box and say, "You want to go to lunch?" or... "We still on for a two o'clock tee time?" Women, on the other hand, can have their day turned upside down because somebody in their cooking class made fun of their shoes, purse, earrings, necklace, makeup, or... and they are irritated the rest of the day. Furthermore, if the woman who spoke out in criticism or ridicule were to suggest that they go to lunch... well... actually, forget that analogy... because it would never happen. Women, again, are wired very differently from men. As relates to conversation, wives need to talk, but they also need a listener. Just like you can have a wife comply with sex that she clearly communicates holds no interest or enjoyment for her, but she fulfills her duty to you in a way that completely undermines the joy of the moment, so men, even when they stop to talk to their wife, or stop to listen to her... may communicate the same spirit of meeting the letter of the law but clearly having no heart in it. When one ear and one eye is on the TV and the ballgame that you are watching, and one eye and one ear is attempting to placate your wife by "listening," you have robbed her of the joy of sharing and communication. Men, your wives need your undivided attention for a reasonable period of time. Make time to talk to her. Understand how much your sharing with her feeds her spirit. And men, learn to be a better listener. Most of us fall short at this point, but we can all improve. It doesn't mean that you need to start saying 25,000 words a day or spend hours listening to the exclusion of your ballgames, your favorite TV show, your favorite hobby, or sport. It does mean that the same principles of **self-sacrifice** and **self-discipline** are needed as you relate to your wife. The same principles as you can rightfully expect from her when it comes to your sexual needs.

As we consider the passages above, how do we apply them to the other needs of men and women? What are some other needs that we should consider?

Well, so far we have discussed and described that men need sex and women need conversation. What else do women desire? They desire **non-sexual affection**. What is that meant to include? It is meant to include the need to be touched in a way that communicates love and appreciation without the ulterior motive of sexual activity. It is hand-holding, it is a foot massage, it is a back rub. It is opening the car door on her side ... like you probably did when you were dating. It is a card that you write, not Hallmark. It is a little note that is unexpected that says you love her, or are thankful for her. It could be a poem you write for her, or flowers you send, or a houseplant she likes. Men, we all need to be better at expressing our affection. This comes more easily for some than others. You may have been raised in an austere family where affection was never displayed, in any form. But again, our call from the Bible is to be **self-sacrificing** and **self-disciplined! Be both!**

What comes next?

Men - want **physical attractiveness** in their wives. Do they complain when women spend money on makeup, beauty shop appointments, or aerobic exercise class fees? I doubt it! Will they grouse about pedicures and manicures, facials and a merry-go-round of clothes? Maybe, but they will not complain about things that make you look good. They want to be proud of the way their wife looks. They want to be in public and know that other guys are saying to themselves, "Boy, he is married to a good-looking gal!" Unfortunately, women far too often let the excuse of I had (two, three, four...) babies, and this just happens. Well, there is a kernel of truth to that, but if you gain 80 or 100 lbs. with pregnancy and have a 6-lb. baby, you are obviously going in the wrong direction! Once the weight is in place, it is much harder to lose than it is to prevent ever getting there. It has always been curious to me that the first thing most women who get divorced do is to lose weight. Why should that be? Keep yourself attractive, not only for your husband but for you! As a physician, I can assure you that nothing good comes from carrying a lot of extra weight. Health issues begin to domino as you age slowly, but surely robs you of reserve in your body systems, and weight dramatically accelerates the process. Men, the same thing applies to you. It is a common phenomenon that men become obese, then have a heart attack, and only then do they get serious and join a gym and do regular exercise and lose weight. Sadly the heart damage is already done, and physical ability is already diminished to rarely be recovered. Why not work to stay in shape and prevent the heart attack, the stroke, the high blood pressure, or the diabetes before it ever happens?

Next in what women tend to want is **openness, honesty**, and **financial support**. Openness and honesty do not need much explanation. If a husband and a wife cannot or will not be honest with each other, they have a poor foundation upon which to build a relationship. Honesty is not just the absence of lying. Honesty is being transparent. Honesty is disclosing use of time or talent or money that you both have a stake in preserving or using. Honestly and openness means lovingly informing your spouse of appearance or behavior issues that negatively impact either your relationship or reflect badly on themselves in the view of others. Gentleness and sensitivity are necessary here. Openness means sharing things and circumstances and even thoughts with your spouse without being asked, prodded, or demanded. Again, "Do unto others as you would have them do unto you."

Financial support is important to most women, because they are wired to build and protect the nest, and to do so takes money. This need is not that women have a dollar amount in mind that they require to be happy, but rather the need to feel secure that the money necessary to carry out their tasks will be there. It is stressful to a woman to have to worry not only about clean clothes for the kids or what she is going to fix for supper, but also whether there is money to buy groceries, clothes, or other necessary items. This responsibility falls principally upon the husband. God has made the man the head of the family, but he has also made man responsible for providing for the family. **Proverbs 31** gives us insight into the fact that wives are expected to be industrious and contribute to the welfare of their family, but the primary responsibility still rests with the husband. We will delve into the subject of finances more in depth later on in this series.

What else was on the list?

Recreational companionship. This can take as many forms as there are people. One couple may think of recreation as a day spent in an art gallery or a museum. For others it may mean being at the deer camp together, or going fishing, golfing, bicycling or simply walking. The point of the need for recreational companionship is that particularly for men, there is great joy in having a wife who expresses interest in their interests and makes way to share in the joy of those experiences. Why is it left to the wife to join her husband in his activities? It is back to Genesis, again! God has tasked you women with the role of being a helper and helpmate **suitable** for him. To be suitable, you can't hate and ignore everything that he enjoys and desires to pursue, and then be surprised that he does not gush with affection and conversation. Again, ladies, see your role as being a facilitator in helping your husband thrive, achieve, and be all that he can be. In the short term you may feel like you are giving up something, but I can assure you, both from personal observation, from sociological data, and from the principles of God's Word that we have discussed, that you will be doing yourself a big favor if you have a happy, satisfied, productive, fulfilled husband who feels loved and valued.

Men, it is time to pick on you again. The next item on our list is **domestic support.** What does this entail? It means that you don't consider it "the little woman's job" when things need to be done around the house. This may involve the mundane, such as taking out the trash. It may involve picking up your own trash, your own dirty clothes, or maybe even doing the laundry or taking care of the children. Too many couples even within the church have a husband who projects the attitude, "Well, I work and provide for the family, so when I get home, I deserve to do what I want." They are oblivious to the overwhelming number of tasks that they are expecting from their wife, who very likely is also working outside of the home. Men often label any of the home duties as "women's work" and feel that as long as they mow the grass, they are doing all that should be expected of them. Once again, we revisit the concept of **self-sacrifice** and **self-discipline.** Open your eyes, men, to the joy of serving your wife and looking for ways to meet her needs. You will find she is much more receptive to you later in the evening when her heart is stirred by your willingness to take care of tasks around the house ... especially if she has not had to ask, beg, or nag to get you to do them.

This follows closely to **family commitment,** although they differ. There is bonding and strength in a family unit when there is visible and consistent priority given to the family. This need is often fumbled more by men than by women. It is so easy to get caught up in the rat race of job and career, the desire for promotion and the legitimate need for recreation, and let family needs take a backseat. Fathers often fail to appreciate the impact that being there for your children at important events in their life and demonstrating to them how much of a priority they are to your life will have on their self-esteem and their quest for affirmation. That need for affirmation may well come from the dope head at school who gives your daughter attention that she really wants from you, but will accept a cheap substitute to try and fill the empty void in her life because you never make time for her. You don't acknowledge her achievement or appearance, or her character qualities that you desire to see in her life. Again, fathers … someone else will fill that void … and you may not like the choice your children make trying to feel valued.

Only one more item is on the list for discussion, and that is **admiration**. This is a need experienced by both males and females, but is inherently more likely in men than in women. You may ask why I say that it is inherently more likely in men, and that again takes us back to the Bible. God initially created man that His glory might be revealed, and that He might be worshipped as He deserves to be. God wanted to be praised and worshipped by his creation. He could have created robots, but he chose to give man the freedom of choice. God wants admiration, and since he told us in Genesis that we were created in His image, it would follow that just like God, we desire to be admired. Since man is closer to being in the mold of the father, it would also follow that men are more likely to desire admiration than women who, under God's direction, see themselves as a helper and helpmate. They don't expect or need to be admired as much as men. Again, women may look at this need as frivolous and unnecessary, but men by and large want to be admired. They want to be admired for what they accomplish, what they build, what they create, what they achieve. Even if you women don't see or understand the need, make it a point to give your husband clear messages of admiration. How important is this? It is easily demonstrated that when men come home to a wife who expresses her admiration for his hard work and faithful provisions, that when she meets his sexual needs and brags on his accomplishments, he will be a happy and satisfied man no matter his station in life. Want proof? Go out to Sanitation Solutions (a local trash collection company) and talk to some of the guys who throw trash on the back of a trash truck. From the standpoint of a social ladder, they are on the bottom rung. And yet, if you find the guy who everyone agrees is the best trash slinger in the organization and whose wife brags that her husband is the fastest and has the most stamina of any trash slinger in the company, and she expresses her admiration, both verbally as well as sexually … you can write it down that that is a happy and fulfilled man, despite being on the bottom of the social ladder. Contrast that man with a billionaire hedge fund manager who goes home to a wife who is self-absorbed and more interested in her social calendar than her husband. A woman who has bought in to the women's rights movement that says she should do what she wants and that submission is demeaning and is to be condemned, and so her husband is deprived of admiration and appreciative sex, and as a result he is miserable and depressed and not uncommonly finds himself over-indulging in alcohol, cocaine, heroin, or in affairs. He simply is looking for something or someone to stop the pain. By now you know what I am going to say. We again have the opportunity to demonstrate **self-sacrifice** and **self-discipline** by giving to our spouse what we ourselves may not need, but in the interest of meeting the needs of our spouse, we generously give admiration and appreciation.

We have now covered the ten aspects of marital needs and have emphasized two of the three primary reasons why couples divorce, namely sex and communication. That leaves us with one remaining primary reason why couples divorce, and that is money.

CHAPTER FIVE

As promised earlier, we will look more specifically at what the Bible has to say about money and how it should be managed within a marriage. The first question that comes to mind is:

* **Why does money lead to divorce?**

Secondarily:

* **Is it the lack of money that causes divorce?**

No, it is not the lack of money that leads to divorce: it is the incompatibility of two people and their view of money! Once again, **it is rigged!** Chances are good that you and your spouse have a different view of money. What do I mean by that? I mean that it is likely that:

* one is a saver	* one is a spender
* one is "thrifty"	* one is extravagant
* one loves to buy on credit	* one only buys when you have the cash
* one looks at debt as just a necessary part of life	* one is driven to be debt-free
* one likes a lot of entertainment and eating out.	* one is reluctant to "waste" money on entertainment or eating out.

*one likes the top brands	*one is happy to get by with function
one likes to spend the moon on Christmas and birthdays	one feels like a card or a call should suffice
*one wants a new(er) car to drive	*one is happy to drive an old vehicle to avoid having payments.
*one wants the most house we can qualify to buy	*one wants to keep payments as low as possible

None of the above illustrations is dependent on the **amount** of money, but rather on the **use** of money. Conflicts arise when the differences are not bridged in a mutually satisfying way. Can you see any likelihood of conflict in the above illustrations? Are you and your spouse wired the same way when it comes to money?

So does the Bible have anything to say about money? Has God or His Son addressed this critical area of marriage? Fortunately, **yes**! Once again, God has been faithful to give His children instruction and direction for their journey through life.

There are four primary principles about money that I think can be found in the teaching of the Bible.

PRINCIPLE #1-

It all belongs to God!

He and He alone has provided you with everything you have!

James 1:17-18

17 Every good and perfect gift is from above, coming down from the Father of the heavenly lights, who does not change like shifting shadows.

1 Cor 4:7

7 For who makes you different from anyone else? What do you have that you did not receive? And if you did receive it, why do you boast as though you did not?

Ps 24:1

24 The earth is the Lord's, and everything in it, the world, and all who live in it;

Rom 11:36

36 For from him and through him and to him are all things. To him be the glory forever! Amen.

Deut 8:18

18 But remember the Lord your God, for it is he who gives you the ability to produce wealth, and so confirms his covenant, which he swore to your forefathers, as it is today.

---

1 Chron 29:12–13

12 Wealth and honor come from you; you are the ruler of all things.

In your hands are strength and power
to exalt and give strength to all.
13 Now, our God, we give you thanks,
and praise your glorious name.

---

1 Sam 2:7–8

7 The Lord sends poverty and wealth;
he humbles and he exalts.
8 He raises the poor from the dust
and lifts the needy from the ash heap;
he seats them with princes
and has them inherit a throne of honor.

Job 42:10–11

10 After Job had prayed for his friends, the Lord made him
prosperous again and gave him twice as much as he had
before.

Prov 8:18–21

18 With me are riches and honor,
enduring wealth and prosperity.
19 My fruit is better than fine gold;
what I yield surpasses choice silver.
20 I walk in the way of righteousness,
along the paths of justice,

21 bestowing wealth on those who love me
and making their treasuries full.

Prov 10:22

22 The blessing of the Lord brings wealth,
and he adds no trouble to it.

Eccl 5:19

19 Moreover, when God gives any man wealth and possessions,
and enables him to enjoy them, to accept his lot and be happy
in his work—this is a gift of God.

Rom 11:35–36

35 "Who has ever given to God,
that God should repay him?"
36 For from him and through him and to him are all things.
To him be the glory forever! Amen.

PRINCIPLE #2 -

God wants us to be givers not takers, and not hoarders!

Deut 15:10–11

10 Give generously to him and do so without a grudging heart; then because of this the Lord your God will bless you in all your work and in everything you put your hand to. 11 There will always be poor people in the land. Therefore I command you to be openhanded toward your brothers and toward the poor and needy in your land.

Luke 6:38

38 Give, and it will be given to you. A good measure, pressed down, shaken together and running over, will be poured into your lap. For with the measure you use, it will be measured to you."

John 3:16–17

16 "For God so loved the world that he gave his one and only Son, that whoever believes in him shall not perish but have eternal life.

Prov 11:24–26

24 One man gives freely, yet gains even more;
another withholds unduly, but comes to poverty.
25 A generous man will prosper;
he who refreshes others will himself be refreshed.
26 People curse the man who hoards grain,
but blessing crowns him who is willing to sell.

Prov 19:17

17 He who is kind to the poor lends to the Lord,
and he will reward him for what he has done.

Prov 22:9

9 A generous man will himself be blessed,
for he shares his food with the poor.

Heb 13:16

16 And do not forget to do good and to share with others, for
with such sacrifices God is pleased.

James 5:1–5

5 Now listen, you rich people, weep and wail because of the
misery that is coming upon you. 2 Your wealth has rotted, and

moths have eaten your clothes. 3 Your gold and silver are corroded. Their corrosion will testify against you and eat your flesh like fire. You have hoarded wealth in the last days. 4 Look! The wages you failed to pay the workmen who mowed your fields are crying out against you. The cries of the harvesters have reached the ears of the Lord Almighty. 5 You have lived on earth in luxury and self-indulgence. You have fattened yourselves in the day of slaughter.

---

2 Cor 9:6–8

6 Remember this: Whoever sows sparingly will also reap sparingly, and whoever sows generously will also reap generously. 7 Each man should give what he has decided in his heart to give, not reluctantly or under compulsion, for God loves a cheerful giver.

These verses speak the truth without having to add to it. God's Word is very clear on this subject. **Be a giver!** *You can't outgive God!*

PRINCIPLE #3 -

God asks us to give tithes and offerings.

Lev 27:30–33

30 "'A tithe of everything from the land, whether grain from the soil or fruit from the trees, belongs to the Lord; it is holy to the Lord. 31 If a man redeems any of his tithe, he must add a fifth of the value to it. 32 The entire tithe of the herd and flock — every tenth animal that passes under the shepherd's rod — will be holy to the Lord. 33 He must not pick out the

good from the bad or make any substitution. If he does make a substitution, both the animal and its substitute become holy and cannot be redeemed.'"

Deut 12:5–7

But you are to seek the place the Lord your God will choose from among all your tribes to put his Name there for his dwelling. To that place you must go; 6 there bring your burnt offerings and sacrifices, your tithes and special gifts, what you have vowed to give and your freewill offerings, and the firstborn of your herds and flocks. 7 There, in the presence of the Lord your God, you and your families shall eat and shall rejoice in everything you have put your hand to, because the Lord your God has blessed you.

Mal 3:8-12

8 "Will a man rob God? Yet you rob me.
"But you ask, 'How do we rob you?'
"In tithes and offerings.
9 You are under a curse—the whole nation of you—because you are robbing me. 10 Bring the whole tithe into the storehouse, that there may be food in my house. Test me in this," says the Lord Almighty, "and see if I will not throw open the floodgates of heaven and pour out so much blessing that you will not have room enough for it. 11 I will prevent pests from devouring your crops, and the vines in your fields will not cast their fruit," says the Lord Almighty. 12 "Then all the nations

will call you blessed, for yours will be a delightful land," says the Lord Almighty.

1 Cor 16:1–4

16 Now about the collection for God's people: Do what I told the Galatian churches to do. 2 On the first day of every week, each one of you should set aside a sum of money in keeping with his income, saving it up, so that when I come no collections will have to be made. 3 Then, when I arrive, I will give letters of introduction to the men you approve and send them with your gift to Jerusalem.

---

2 Cor 8:7

But just as you excel in everything—in faith, in speech, in knowledge, in complete earnestness and in your love for us— see that you also excel in this grace of giving.

---

2 Cor 9:6-15

6 Remember this: Whoever sows sparingly will also reap sparingly, and whoever sows generously will also reap generously. 7 Each man should give what he has decided in his heart to give, not reluctantly or under compulsion, for God loves a cheerful giver. 8 And God is able to make all grace abound to you, so that in all things at all times, having all that you need, you will abound in every good work. 9 As it is written:
"He has scattered abroad his gifts to the poor;
his righteousness endures forever."

10 Now he who supplies seed to the sower and bread for food will also supply and increase your store of seed and will enlarge the harvest of your righteousness. 11 You will be made rich in every way so that you can be generous on every occasion, and through us your generosity will result in thanksgiving to God. 12 This service that you perform is not only supplying the needs of God's people but is also overflowing in many expressions of thanks to God. 13 Because of the service by which you have proved yourselves, men will praise God for the obedience that accompanies your confession of the gospel of Christ, and for your generosity in sharing with them and with everyone else. 14 And in their prayers for you their hearts will go out to you, because of the surpassing grace God has given you. 15 Thanks be to God for his indescribable gift!

Prov 3:9–10

9 Honor the Lord with your wealth,
with the firstfruits of all your crops;
10 then your barns will be filled to overflowing,
and your vats will brim over with new wine.

No, tithing is not just an old testament command. It is intended in the New Testament that we will tithe and give offerings out of a **"heart of love"** and out of "Thanksgiving."

PRINCIPLE #4 -

"Invest" where wealth is eternal and not temporal!

Matt 6:19-21

19 "Do not store up for yourselves treasures on earth, where moth and rust destroy, and where thieves break in and steal. 20 But store up for yourselves treasures in heaven, where moth and rust do not destroy, and where thieves do not break in and steal. 21 For where your treasure is, there your heart will be also.

Mark 10:29-31

29 "I tell you the truth," Jesus replied, "no one who has left home or brothers or sisters or mother or father or children or fields for me and the gospel 30 will fail to receive a hundred times as much in this present age (homes, brothers, sisters, mothers, children and fields — and with them, persecutions) and in the age to come, eternal life.

---

1 Tim 6:6-10

6 But godliness with contentment is great gain. 7 For we brought nothing into the world, and we can take nothing out of it. 8 But if we have food and clothing, we will be content with that. 9 People who want to get rich fall into temptation and a trap and into many foolish and harmful desires that plunge men into ruin and destruction. 10 For the love of money is a root of

all kinds of evil. Some people, eager for money, have wandered from the faith and pierced themselves with many griefs.

1 Tim 6:17–19

17 Command those who are rich in this present world not to be arrogant nor to put their hope in wealth, which is so uncertain, but to put their hope in God, who richly provides us with everything for our enjoyment. 18 Command them to do good, to be rich in good deeds, and to be generous and willing to share. 19 In this way they will lay up treasure for themselves as a firm foundation for the coming age, so that they may take hold of the life that is truly life.

Eccl 5:13–20

13 I have seen a grievous evil under the sun:
wealth hoarded to the harm of its owner,
14 or wealth lost through some misfortune,
so that when he has a son
there is nothing left for him.
15 Naked a man comes from his mother's womb,
and as he comes, so he departs.
He takes nothing from his labor
that he can carry in his hand.
16 This too is a grievous evil:
As a man comes, so he departs,
and what does he gain,
since he toils for the wind?
17 All his days he eats in darkness,
with great frustration, affliction and anger.

18 Then I realized that it is good and proper for a man to eat and drink, and to find satisfaction in his toilsome labor under the sun during the few days of life God has given him — for this is his lot. 19 Moreover, when God gives any man wealth and possessions, and enables him to enjoy them, to accept his lot and be happy in his work — this is a gift of God. 20 He seldom reflects on the days of his life, because God keeps him occupied with gladness of heart.

These four principles are easily understood from God's Word. Take time to reflect on how each of these principles speak to you, and what changes you need to make in your life to be in conformity with God's Word.

As we are nearing the conclusion of this series, let me leave you with some take-home messages and applications about money:

1) **Develop a plan for money management** that is commensurate with scripture and acceptable to both of you. God gives foundational truths, but you have a lot of latitude. Talk openly and honestly about money issues with your spouse. If you have been struggling with developing a plan, I would encourage you to take the Dave Ramsey Money Management Course.

2) Money is once again an opportunity for you to **learn to "give up rights,"** to be a blessing to others. Remember: *God's primary objective for each one of us is to become more like Christ*. Consider the story of Ananias and Sapphira in Acts chapter 5. They valued money above honesty, praise more than deceit. Their deaths were not punishment because they had kept some money for themselves, but because they lied to God and sought the praise of men while wanting to hoard money.

3) **Avoid Debt** - My recommendation is ideally to remain debt-free. Recognizing that it is not always possible to avoid debt—enter

into debt only for things that *appreciate* in value (in other words, things whose value tends to rise over time)

4) **Learn to live within your means** - Do not try and keep up with anybody else. Do not be in a hurry to live the life you **expect** to have someday rather than the life you have today. Remember:

Heb 13:5

5 Keep your lives free from the love of money and be content with what you have, because God has said,
"Never will I leave you; never will I forsake you."

---

1 Tim 6:8–10

8 But if we have food and clothing, we will be content with that. 9 People who want to get rich fall into temptation and a trap and into many foolish and harmful desires that plunge men into ruin and destruction. 10 For the love of money is a root of all kinds of evil. Some people, eager for money, have wandered from the faith and pierced themselves with many griefs.

Phil 4:11–13

11 I am not saying this because I am in need, for I have learned to be content whatever the circumstances. 12 I know what it is to be in need, and I know what it is to have plenty. I have learned the secret of being content in any and every situation, whether well fed or hungry, whether living in plenty or in want. 13 I can do everything through him who gives me strength.

5) **Pay tithe first!** Then see what else you have to spend. **Don't** spend and then see if there is any left for God or church.

6) **Pay yourself second!** - Put 10 percent of your income into savings and investments.

7) **Maintain an emergency three-month reserve.**

8) **Talk** to your spouse about money management and come to a mutually agreeable position, even if it is a compromise for both of you.

9) **Hold on to money loosely!** Be prepared and open to give to those in need; use money to minister to others as Christ's ambassador.

So this concludes the foundation that I wanted to be sure you all have. A foundation based squarely on the principles found in God's Word. To put this whole series into perspective, let me try to tie it all together and pick up the threads that run all the way through our series.

#1 - Understand that marriage is rigged! Rigged by God *by design!* God does not want you to be happy so much as He wants you to be Godly! And how does He make you Godly? He uses the sandpaper of marital difference to force you to learn to be **self-disciplined** and **self-sacrificing**. That is because these two character qualities are the most emblematic of Jesus Christ himself.

#2 - Do you understand and see now that the fact that your mate is so different from you is by design? Do you recognize that whether we are talking about money, sex, or communication, the differences will require compromise and yielding of rights if both of you are to be fulfilled in the relationship? And by the way, if you have had a spouse who has always yielded to you and you have always had your way, I hate to tell you but you won't be happy, and your spouse will harbor anger and resentment. You will never experience the sweetness of unity, harmony, and true "oneness" unless you have learned **self-discipline** and **self-sacrifice**.

#3 - One of the great truths that I want you to take away from this series is the authority hierarchy. In understanding this hierarchy, you need to understand that God has made a special provision and protection for the weakest and lowest in the authority chain.

Jer 49:11

11 Leave your orphans; I will protect their lives.
Your widows too can trust in me."

James 1:27

27 Religion that God our Father accepts as pure and faultless is this: to look after orphans and widows in their distress and to keep oneself from being polluted by the world.

These verses attest to God's provision.

1 Cor 12:12–31

12 The body is a unit, though it is made up of many parts; and though all its parts are many, they form one body. So it is with Christ. 13 For we were all baptized by one Spirit into one body — whether Jews or Greeks, slave or free — and we were all given the one Spirit to drink.
14 Now the body is not made up of one part but of many. 15 If the foot should say, "Because I am not a hand, I do not belong to the body," it would not for that reason cease to be part of the body. 16 And if the ear should say, "Because I am not an eye, I do not belong to the body," it would not for that reason cease to be part of the body. 17 If the whole body were an eye, where would the sense of hearing be? If the whole body were an ear, where would the sense of smell be? 18 But in fact God has

arranged the parts in the body, every one of them, just as he wanted them to be. 19 If they were all one part, where would the body be? 20 As it is, there are many parts, but one body.

21 The eye cannot say to the hand, "I don't need you!" And the head cannot say to the feet, "I don't need you!" 22 On the contrary, those parts of the body that seem to be weaker are indispensable, 23 and the parts that we think are less honorable we treat with special honor. And the parts that are unpresentable are treated with special modesty, 24 while our presentable parts need no special treatment. But God has combined the members of the body and has given greater honor to the parts that lacked it, 25 so that there should be no division in the body, but that its parts should have equal concern for each other. 26 If one part suffers, every part suffers with it; if one part is honored, every part rejoices with it.

27 Now you are the body of Christ, and each one of you is a part of it. 28 And in the church God has appointed first of all apostles, second prophets, third teachers, then workers of miracles, also those having gifts of healing, those able to help others, those with gifts of administration, and those speaking in different kinds of tongues. 29 Are all apostles? Are all prophets? Are all teachers? Do all work miracles? 30 Do all have gifts of healing? Do all speak in tongues? Do all interpret? 31 But eagerly desire the greater gifts.

And now I will show you the most excellent way.

Gal 3:28–29

28 There is neither Jew nor Greek, slave nor free, male nor female, for you are all one in Christ Jesus.

Both of these last two scripture passages clearly reveal that God sees males and females as "equal" but "different." Whether we are talking about the authority hierarchy of God the Father->God the Son->God the Holy Spirit->Man->Woman->children or whether we are talking about the hierarchy of the church and the body of Christ; namely, Christ->apostles->prophets->teachers->workers of miracles->gifts of healing->those who help others->gifts of administration-> then speaking in tongues. Christ makes it plain that even though there are robust differences in His body, the church, we are all equal. Marriage, as we stated early on, is simply a physical manifestation of the spiritual characteristics of Christ's body, the church. The marriage body, while composed of different parts: husband, wife, daughter, daughter-in-law, son, son-in-law, children, parents, grandparents, great grandparents... there is still the possibility of unity and oneness that God desires.

#4 - And last but not least, this series has been about gaining a greater understanding of what it means to love. To understand true love, we only have to look at Jesus Christ, whom scripture declares to **be** LOVE. Scripture declares:

John 1:1–5

1 In the beginning was the Word, and the Word was with God, and the Word was God. 2 He was with God in the beginning. 3 Through him all things were made; without him nothing was made that has been made. 4 In him was life, and that life was the light of men. 5 The light shines in the darkness, but the darkness has not understood it.

John 1:10–14

10 He was in the world, and though the world was made through him, the world did not recognize him. 11 He came to that which was his own, but his own did not receive him. 12 Yet to all who received him, to those who believed in his name, he gave the right to become children of God—13 children born not of natural descent, nor of human decision or a husband's will, but born of God.

14 The Word became flesh and made his dwelling among us. We have seen his glory, the glory of the One and Only, who came from the Father, full of grace and truth.

---

1 John 2:3–6

3 We know that we have come to know him if we obey his commands. 4 The man who says, "I know him," but does not do what he commands is a liar, and the truth is not in him. 5 But if anyone obeys his word, God's love is truly made complete in him. This is how we know we are in him: 6 Whoever claims to live in him must walk as Jesus did.

---

1 John 2:15–17

15 Do not love the world or anything in the world. If anyone loves the world, the love of the Father is not in him. 16 For everything in the world — the cravings of sinful man, the lust of his eyes and the boasting of what he has and does — comes not from the Father but from the world. 17 The world and its

desires pass away, but the man who does the will of God lives forever.

---

1 John 3:16–24

16 This is how we know what love is: Jesus Christ laid down his life for us. And we ought to lay down our lives for our brothers. 17 If anyone has material possessions and sees his brother in need but has no pity on him, how can the love of God be in him? 18 Dear children, let us not love with words or tongue but with actions and in truth. 19 This then is how we know that we belong to the truth, and how we set our hearts at rest in his presence 20 whenever our hearts condemn us. For God is greater than our hearts, and he knows everything.

21 Dear friends, if our hearts do not condemn us, we have confidence before God 22 and receive from him anything we ask, because we obey his commands and do what pleases him. 23 And this is his command: to believe in the name of his Son, Jesus Christ, and to love one another as he commanded us. 24 Those who obey his commands live in him, and he in them. And this is how we know that he lives in us: We know it by the Spirit he gave us.

---

1 John 4:7-12

7 Dear friends, let us love one another, for love comes from God. Everyone who loves has been born of God and knows God. 8 Whoever does not love does not know God, because God is love. 9 This is how God showed his love among us: He sent his one and only Son into the world that we might live

through him. 10 This is love: not that we loved God, but that he loved us and sent his Son as an atoning sacrifice for our sins. 11 Dear friends, since God so loved us, we also ought to love one another. 12 No one has ever seen God; but if we love one another, God lives in us and his love is made complete in us.

---

1 John 4:16–21

16 And so we know and rely on the love God has for us. God is love. Whoever lives in love lives in God, and God in him. 17 In this way, love is made complete among us so that we will have confidence on the day of judgment, because in this world we are like him. 18 There is no fear in love. But perfect love drives out fear, because fear has to do with punishment. The one who fears is not made perfect in love. 19 We love because he first loved us. 20 If anyone says, "I love God," yet hates his brother, he is a liar. For anyone who does not love his brother, whom he has seen, cannot love God, whom he has not seen. 21 And he has given us this command: Whoever loves God must also love his brother.

---

1 John 5:3–5

3 This is love for God: to obey his commands. And his commands are not burdensome, 4 for everyone born of God overcomes the world. This is the victory that has overcome the world, even our faith. 5 Who is it that overcomes the world? Only he who believes that Jesus is the Son of God.

So, we can close out our time together by one more scriptural definition of love—the most poignant and pointed description of love in all of world literature;

1 Cor 13

13 If I speak in the tongues of men and of angels, but have not love, I am only a resounding gong or a clanging cymbal. 2 If I have the gift of prophecy and can fathom all mysteries and all knowledge, and if I have a faith that can move mountains, but have not love, I am nothing. 3 If I give all I possess to the poor and surrender my body to the flames, but have not love, I gain nothing.
4 Love is patient, love is kind. It does not envy, it does not boast, it is not proud. 5 It is not rude, it is not self-seeking, it is not easily angered, it keeps no record of wrongs. 6 Love does not delight in evil but rejoices with the truth. 7 It always protects, always trusts, always hopes, always perseveres.
8 Love never fails. But where there are prophecies, they will cease; where there are tongues, they will be stilled; where there is knowledge, it will pass away. 9 For we know in part and we prophesy in part, 10 but when perfection comes, the imperfect disappears. 11 When I was a child, I talked like a child, I thought like a child, I reasoned like a child. When I became a man, I put childish ways behind me. 12 Now we see but a poor reflection as in a mirror; then we shall see face to face. Now I know in part; then I shall know fully, even as I am fully known. 13 And now these three remain: faith, hope and love. But the greatest of these is love.

I implore you by the power of God's Word to live with each other in love. Not in romantic, Hollywood love, but in true agape love as modeled by Jesus Christ. Love in the four dimensions that Christ himself defined—emotionally, physically, intellectually, and spiritually. If you do, I can promise you, on the strength of God's Word, that you will have a blessed relationship in which Christ is honored and pleased, in which you become more like Christ and in which Christ can bless you with all of the fruit of the Spirit: **love, joy, peace, patience, kindness, goodness, faithfulness, gentleness, and self-control.** Galatians 5:22

God bless you for your interest in this series. As I express every time I teach, the final conclusion I want to leave you with is this:

Living life God's way
is the <u>only</u> way
to live without regret!

In Christ's love, this series has been written and compiled
by
Donald L. Wikoff, MD
that marriages who pursue these truths might experience all that
God intended and designed for marriage to become.
God bless you!

Maximize Your Marriage!

According to God's plan as presented in scripture

Bible passages related to marriage, some more directly related than others but providing the primary basis for a Biblical view of marriage. Read, ponder, assimilate, and instigate to maximize marriage. God bless you in your endeavor!

(Arranged in Biblical order)

Genesis 1:26–28 (creation of man; also 5:1, 2)
2:18–25 (creation of woman, marriage ordained)
3:16–19 (the curse on woman and man for their sin)

Proverbs 5:15 (15–23 are a warning against adultery)
5:18, 19
12:4 (wife of noble character versus disgraceful wife)
14:1 (wise/foolish woman)
18:22 (a wife is a good favor from the Lord)
19:14 (a prudent wife is from the Lord)
31:10–31 (a wife of noble character)

Song of Solomon - the entire book!

Malachi   2:14–15 (children - God desires Godly offspring)

1 Cor. 7:1–9 (and even 1–40, i.e., all of chapter 7) marital expectations

11:3–10 (propriety in worship)

13:1–13 **LOVE** chapter

14:34 (women should not speak in church)

Ephesians 5:22, 23

Colossians 3:18–25 (rules for Christian households)

1 Timothy 2:12–15 (instruction for worship - role of man/woman)

5:1–16 (about widows)

Titus   2:1–5 or (1–8) (what to teach men/women both old and young)

1 Peter   3:1–12 (wives - be submissive; husbands - live with your wife in a manner where your prayers won't be hindered)

Read, reread, and study these passages as you ask the Holy Spirit to shed light on the truth He has for you in these verses.

www.ingramcontent.com/pod-product-compliance
Ingram Content Group UK Ltd.
Pitfield, Milton Keynes, MK11 3LW, UK
UKHW020813120325
456141UK00001B/80